MW01092400

HOW TO GET

A DEGREE

IN CELIBACY

10 STEPS TO KEEPING YOUR LIPS CLOSED

BERNICE L. WOODEN

To: Goddess Vanessa!

Page Left Intentionally Blank

Thank you for loving me. Watching your dreams coming true is amazing!

ISBN: 978-1536828214

Book Cover Design by Demarcus McGaughey

Book Format by Lauren Varlack

Author photo by Xanda Tonge

Visit me on the web! www.bernicewooden.com

Dedication

This book is dedicated to those who are redefining their lives through celibacy and abstinence. May your journey be full of healing, joy, and happiness.

Ashe

CONTENTS

Part I: THE WHY'S

Part II: THE WORK

Part III: THE WAIT

INTRODUCTION

Through this candid account of true stories, I share intimate details that lead to my journey of celibacy. This book will guide those who may decide a similar path and how to be empowered through the process. I hope my stories remind you of all of the fun conversations you've had with your BFF's about love and life.

While celibacy and abstinence become more popular in our culture, it is only right to enhance the experience with a positive outlook. Celibacy is a choice of love, reflection, and self-awareness. I promise you'll enjoy this book as much as I did writing it for you. Hashtag your questions to me by using: #Adegreeincelibacy.

Let the journey begin...

*** *Names have been changed to respect the privacy of those involved in the stories shared in this book.*

BE FREE

My womb seeks truth

It is generating questions and doubts

I must dig deep into my soul, pull at the root

Who can I love?

How can I live when the fight is within?

Her touch is gracious

His body is carved like ample drops of fine wine

Where can I go to free my mind?

Spending time with her

Loving her

Touching her majestic curves soothes the love within

His face is a reminder of the future

How can I love?

When can I live when the fight is within?

Treasured memories spark new life

New joys create a profound view

I am finally me

It is time to be free

Part I:
THE
WHY'S

Chapter One

LESSON ONE

"I do my best because I'm counting on you counting on me."

-Maya Angelou

· · · · · ·  · · · · · ·

The bathroom is where it all started. No really, it did. At the age of three my mother taught me a few things, and most of the time, my lessons were lectured while I played in the sink. My first lesson was about self-love. Of course, at the young age of three years old, I didn't know what self-love was, but my mother taught me one day.

She followed me into the bathroom and picked me up so I could face the mirror. My small feet stood inside the bathroom sink as my mother held me tight. She told me to repeat the words she was saying and to look at my reflection. She started projecting her voice with words of encouragement like, "I am beautiful, I am smart." I would repeat after her, "I am beautiful, I am smart." She would then continue, "I am a leader, I am great!" I of course repeated the words with passion when she would make me iterate them if she didn't believe me. This would go on for about five minutes. She would then ask, "How do you feel?" and I would say, "Happy!" We started that ritual almost every day before school. It is one of the earliest lessons I can remember. The next lesson I recall was about sex.

My mother, a single, hard-working parent, was raising

me alone. We lived in Red Hook Houses, which was coined one of the roughest neighborhoods in the country by *Time Magazine* in 1988. At that age, I remember little bits of information but I will never forget what Momma said one morning.

I first learned about sex at five years old. I was standing on the side of the bathtub brushing my teeth while watching myself in the mirror. She walked into the bathroom with a banana and a small silver packet. She said, "Bernice, I need you to pay attention." As I watched her with curiosity, she ripped open the silver packet and took out this wet rubber thing. She then said, "Bernice, this is a condom. A man should put this on his penis whenever he wants to have sex with you." As I continued watching and not knowing what sex was, I remember saying, "Okay, Mommy." She then slid the condom down the banana and said, "Bernice, I will not always be there to protect you. Just know that you are valuable and never do anything you don't want to do." Again, all I could say as a five year old was, "Okay Mommy," and, as she exited the bathroom, I turned back to the mirror to finish brushing my teeth. It was a moment I will never forget.

Saying Goodbye

As I grew older and started making friends, it was clear that my mother's talks, which always sounded like church sermons, were drilled in my head consciously and unconsciously. I would always think about the consequences from any given situation. People called me a "Teacher's Pet," but I considered myself one smart chick. My mother instilled this fear of disobedience so it's fair to say that I was scared of her. Because of this fear, sex was not an option but it didn't keep me away from having friends who had sex or from listening to their sex stories.

Renee invited me to her boyfriend's house regularly. I was the lingering "third wheel" for most of my teenage years.

It would go something like this: "Hey Bernice, want to go to John's house so we can watch *B.E.T.*?" and I, being the "girl without cable," would always say, "Sure!" Anyhoo, on this day John said, "Let's watch something else before we watch *106 and Park.*" We of course obliged and watched as he grabbed a VHS tape and pressed it firmly into the VCR player. As the video began to play, I couldn't believe my eyes! There I was watching two people having sex on one of the largest wooden TVs I'd ever seen, smack dab in the middle of the living room floor. I covered my eyes while peeking through my skinny fingers to see what was going on. My friend and her boyfriend were laughing at me entirely too hard. I was starting to turn red from embarrassment.

I twisted and turned my body from discomfort even though I was curious to watch. As they giggled and chuckled, what happened next paralyzed me for years. The man ejaculated on the woman's face, and I nearly passed out in shock. I ran to the bathroom to throw up my school lunch and locked myself in the bathroom until they turned the video off. Funny thing is, they weren't in a rush to do it so I was in the bathroom for about 15 minutes brushing my teeth with my finger and screaming obscenities as they laughed louder and louder.

It became quiet in the living room and Renee knocked on the bathroom door. "Bernice, are you okay in there?" I remember shouting, "I hope so. My eyes are forever blinded by the crap on that TV!" She continued to laugh but said, "John turned off the TV so you can come out." I opened the door slowly and made my way back to the living room and as soon as I turned the corner, John unmuted the video and it began to play again. THEY TRICKED ME! I was so pissed off that I finally left the house and marched angrily down five flights of stairs.

After that incident died down, Renee and I started seeing each other less. She started hanging with people I didn't like in Red Hook. They were a bad influence, and we eventually parted ways. I will not lie, it hurt like hell but at that time I had to choose what was right for me. I created new friendships and started focusing all of my energy on school. Because my body matured quite quickly, I had older men whistling at me more frequently. I had 41-inch hips and a small waist that kept guys crushing on me but they knew they never had a shot, especially the boys in Red Hook. My mom always used to say, "Never do your dirt where you lay," so I never really dated anyone from my neighborhood.

High School

Two years later, I was enjoying my new friends at Washington Irving High School. They were pretty open about their sexual escapades... it was quite the thrill to hear them share new stories every week. I would listen quietly with anticipation as stories of meeting during the lunch break and afterschool filled our classrooms in between breaks. For me, it was more fun to hear about it than to experience it. I never really questioned if they were telling the truth or not because the stories they shared were always fun to hear. Now that I look back on it, I am sure much of what I heard were either exaggerations or outright lies.

One of my fondest memories in high school is from a girl who I shared a class with during my junior year. There were ten of us in the classroom waiting for the teacher to arrive. We were joking around and talking about current events when Isabella pulled out a banana (Yeah, I know, enough with these banana stories.) She however was going to do something totally different from what my Mother did. One of the guys from our class made a bet with her. I can remember clear as day, Sam said, "Isabella, I dare you to deep-throat that banana. If you do it, I'll give you $5 dollars." We all looked at her and wondered what she would say. Without saying a word, she peeled open the longest banana I've ever seen in my life and slowly pushed it down her throat. We were all wide-eyed and fascinated with her "trick." She actually began tearing and choking as the banana filled her esophagus. She then quickly pulled the banana out of her mouth, coughed before she laughed hysterically and snatched that $5 from Sam's desk. We were all quite stunned. She was always one of the smartest girls in the Teaching Department but she was never taken seriously because the boys gave her the wrong attention. She was blunt, outspoken, and sassy; the fellas were always checking for her. Now me? That's another story...

I was one of the class clowns, or so that's what my friends would say. I always had a rebuttal for any and everything. It was my favorite thing to do in the world, make people laugh. While my jokes rarely interrupted learning in the classroom, if I was ever bored, I would write funny jokes on pieces of paper and either throw or pass them to my friends. When I think about it, most of my friends were funny, too! We were all equally intelligent and had a good time together. We were true to the notion: you are who you chose to be around.

As I approached my final year in high school, I officially had my first boyfriend or at least that's what we called each other. He was handsome and hung out with the "cool kids." Andrew approached me one day after school and said he wanted to date me. At the time, I didn't know what to do so I kept saying no. I said no for a few weeks until I finally said yes. We would meet each other after school and walk around the park in Herald Square. He was always respectful until the time I went to his house in Parkchester.

Andrew invited me over one Saturday, so I trekked my way all the way from Red Hook to his place. I remember it being a cool breeze so it definitely had to be spring. He lived with his grandfather who at the time was working so we were alone. I remember the apartment was filled to the brim with items. He shared that his grandfather was a hoarder.

While we made our way to the back of his apartment, I noticed that his room too was filled to capacity. I could tell he was starting to feel embarrassed so I reassured him everything was okay. We sat on the bed and watched TV for a bit. He then proceeded to kiss me. You see, I had absolutely no problem with kissing but he then tried to unbutton my pants, and my mother came right into my mind, *Girl, if you come home pregnant, I am kicking you out!* That image brought me to my senses; I then told him I wasn't ready. He tried again but I was stern the second time around, "No!" He then moved away from me and said we should go for a walk.

As we walked in silence to the park, we sat on a concrete block. He then said to me that he wanted to break up with me. He had a lot on his mind, the corny excuse for breaking up with someone, and he wanted some space. Our two-month high school relationship was over. It was clear to me that he wanted to break up with me because I didn't have sex with him 30 minutes ago, so like the clown I am I said, "Well, I guess sex with you next week is out of the question, awesome!" He then looked at me and asked, "Are you serious?" I played it off well and said, "Of course! The only reason I said no today is because I have a headache but now that I am single, you don't have to worry about that." His jaw dropped. He immediately tried to play it off as though he had been playing around, "Bernice, I was just joking, why would I want to break up with you." It was clear to me that my choice for saying no resulted in our breakup.

The truth is: if he was upset about not having sex with me, imagine all of the other things he would have been upset about. He missed his mark and I was relieved. I was never a pushover and no amount of pressure was going to make me do anything I didn't want to. I guess all of those lectures from my mother did stick. I had bigger fish to fry at 17 years old, and I was ready for the ocean.

CHAPTER TWO

MY FIRST TIME

"It's crazy what you can talk yourself out of when you're scared and into when you're not."

-Missy Welsh

· · · · · ·  · · · · · ·

My mom is one of the most brilliant people on the planet. She may not believe it, but a lot of her mistakes and stories helped shape me into the woman I am today. Subconsciously, the advice I got from my mom while growing up was good enough to prevent me from making mistakes that I would have come to regret.

My mom is such a character. During my teenager years, the conversations about sex grew heavily. She was always anxious to share but nervous to know if I'd had my first sexual experience. One day while attending high school, I came home with a hickey on my neck and she almost died! She thought I was having sex with boys around my neighborhood. The truth is: I wasn't but most of my friends were. The hickey? Well, kissing and touching was something I decided to do at that age. The boy I was kissing moved from my lips to my neck and soon after, I was bruised with his mark.

She scolded me and I listened. That was usually the case at home. My mom would always say, "Make sure your first experience is with someone you love and trust." She also would say, "If you came home pregnant, I'm kicking you out!" so it was clear I wasn't going to have sex anytime soon.

Sidebar: I never really thought she would kick me out if I got pregnant but I damn sure wasn't going to take a chance!

Things soon changed when I met my second boyfriend, Slim.

Slim was the only guy at my job who didn't give me any attention. My co-workers at Dean & Deluca would flirt with me all the time but Slim would greet me and keep it moving. This was a big turn-on (you know how we always want what seems out of reach) and so I decided to make a move on him. One day after work, he invited me to go shopping with him at 34th Street. After about two hours of shopping, we grabbed some food at a nearby pizza shop.

As we sat down and began eating, a homeless woman came over to our table and asked for money. I said no while Slim gave her a dollar. She thanked him and then told him, "She is awful and will lead you to a horrible life." We both laughed as she left the pizza shop. After that nice chuckle, I actually shared that I had feelings for him and would like to be his girlfriend. I remember feeling the butterflies in my stomach and waiting for his answer. At 17 years old, I officially had my first REAL boyfriend. He was a Leo like me but definitely more timid and shy than I was. It was a balance that I enjoyed. It was fun to be in a relationship for the first time. We looked out for each other in many ways and he is the one I decided to lose my virginity to. What I loved most about him is that he never EVER rushed me. He let me choose when I was ready to have my first experience with him.

Sidebar: I would lie to my mom and tell her I was spending the night at my friend Ivy's house. Ivy lived one block away from Slims' apartment in Soundview way up in the Bronx. Ivy, being the good friend that she was, would check in with my mom as I spent time with him (sorry, Mom.)

That evening, he did everything he could to make me comfortable but I was a nervous wreck! After we ate dinner, we both took a shower and watched TV. It was getting pretty late so we decided the time was now. Through his nervousness and my awkwardness, it felt like I'd decided to jump out of a plane! I asked him to turn off the TV because I didn't want to see anything, and I was starting to get annoyed with his nervous behavior. You see: he already had sex. He was three years older than me but he didn't want to make me uncomfortable. He was gentle and loving throughout the entire experience and I was in shock. I had my first sexual experience with the first person I ever fell in love with (thanks Mom for the tip!)

Throughout our three-year relationship, he did the best he could with what he had. We both came from single-parent homes and we both worked hard to get the things we wanted. I went off to college while he worked two jobs but things shifted once I graduated. I was attracted to something more... something more fulfilling and my body yearned to be partnered with someone else. As our three-year flame slowly died out, I knew it was time to branch out and work on what I wanted. At the time, I wanted substance and more affection so I went out on a voyage to find it.

CHAPTER THREE

BOYS, BOYS, AND MORE BOYS

"A kiss that is never tasted is forever and ever wasted."

-Billie Holiday

After my breakup with Slim, I started dating again. Websites like *BlackPlanet* and *Myspace* were a part of my everyday viewing. I also used to jump on the *Chatline* when I was bored. It's crazy how times have changed.

I didn't go on many dates but I do remember two people that I met on *Blackplanet* who were two totally different characters. Omar from Flatbush, was gentle, kind, and lovely and Timothy was cold and distant. Let's talk about Omar first.

Omar was ten years my senior so I never took him seriously. He would say things like, "I love you Bernice and you are going to be my wife" but I would laugh it off thinking about his three daughters and I was way too young to be a step-mother. I had to be around 22 years old at the time. I was actually too scared to have sex with him because I thought he would get me pregnant! I could not bear the thought of having children at that age, so I was very cautious.

One day though, he wanted to chill in a hotel room. At 22, I am old enough to know what his intention was however he guaranteed no sex. I asked, "How can you guarantee there will be no sex?" He then said, "We will only do it if you want to." I felt empowered after he said that and it was the ignition I needed to meet him that weekend. Once I entered the hotel room, I was "shitting bricks" but I did my best to hold my composure. It was a very awkward place to be with someone I didn't consider as a spouse. We then ordered food and watched TV. After we watched a movie, I went into the bathroom to take a shower, and when I came out he was laid out in his underwear. I told him, "I knew it! You are trying to trap me!" He giggled and said, "No I'm not. I am hot so I took my clothes off." *Oh that sucker thinks I'm stupid.* I neatly placed my outside clothes on a chair and climbed into the bed.

We snuggled and started to watch another movie but I knew we wouldn't be getting to the climax of the film because we had our own climax to reach. It's not what you think though. His entire attention was on my pussy. He slowly played with her and I moaned and tried to keep my mind on the movie. He then moved his head down in between my thighs. It would be the first time in my life someone visited "her" face to face besides my gynecologist. Because it was my first time, I started laughing and he asked, "What's wrong?" All I could think about was how nervous I was. All I heard was breathing and licking in places I never imagined until then. It was awesome! He loved what he was doing and I did too. He was brilliant and could teach my future ex-boyfriend's a thing or two.

We continued our "friendship" for four months with a few more "face to face" visits. Believe it or not, we never had sex and he respected my choice. He soon realized that I was not taking him seriously so he decided to end our "friendship." I never considered him my boyfriend because of our age difference, but we enjoyed keeping each other company.

Now Timothy? I was caught up. I used to call him, "East

New York" and he was definitely more than a friend or at least I thought so. He worked at NYU while I was still working at Dean & Deluca. By that time, I have been with the company for five years and was a supervisor at the Paramount Hotel location. Timothy and I went on dates quite often and we spent time together at least twice a week. He would drive to Red Hook to see me and we would hang out at the pier. Though he was cold and came off emotionless, I would always catch him looking at me... right into my soul. It was his eyes and deep, deep velvet voice that created a relationship of powerful sex. And that's all it ever was between us even though I wanted more.

He would invite me over to his house when his male friends were there. They would play video games and I would just watch to be in his presence. He was an outlet through the stress I was feeling as a young adult: bills, bills, and more bills. After an hour of gaming, he would usually end the session and the fellas knew it was time to leave so we could be alone. They would give me a smirk as if they knew Timothy was about to pin me to the couch. I didn't have any shame because I was hooked.

After eight months, I just couldn't take it anymore. Though the sex was amazing, that is all it ever was. I was starting to feel unappreciated and spent most of my time being angry with him. After I ended our eight-month escapade, he would text me things like, "Bernice, I do love you. I wish I would have told you sooner." But by that time it was too late. I had already started mending my broken heart. I couldn't understand how girls my age could jump from one relationship to another without thoroughly reviewing what went wrong and getting over the previous relationship completely.

As I healed through the hurt, I decided I needed a break from relationships. It was the first time I considered celibacy. I was still getting used to the world and what a relationship would look like for me. I decided that it was time for a shift and it all happened swiftly, even the relationship with my mother changed.

While working at a Production Company in Harlem, it was hard to follow my mother's rules due to conflicting schedules with my job. I was hired to host and produce online content which many times involved me attending industry events and staying out late. We started to argue often about my level of respect for her and the house so I left Red Hook.

There I was, moving into my first apartment on Monroe Street in Bedford Stuyvesant in 2007. It was on the third level of a brownstone. It was the perfect space and I was excited. I felt independent and confident. I could finally do what I wanted and lead a life on my own terms. I was able to go to work, come home, and not have anyone to answer to… I was living the good life.

Things changed after nine months when I met Ray. He was someone that I interviewed for the show. He was handsome and nice but I didn't want to mix business with pleasure so I kindly declined his advances that night. The next morning I received a call at my job and guess who was on the other line? I couldn't believe he followed up so fast! He soon showed me what consistency and persistence looked like. We chatted on the phone for a bit but I had to get back to editing a video so I told him I had to go. He asked for my cell phone number and I said no. So what do you think he did next? He called me every day while at work until I finally gave in.

We started talking on the phone quite often. Weeks turned into months and I professed my love for him… through a dare. One of my high school friends Ana and I were on the bus heading back to Bed-Stuy and she was asking me about Ray. I told her that he was a good guy and was patient. He didn't try anything with me, which was always a bonus in my book. He didn't label our relationship yet but it did feel like we were in a relationship. Ana said, "So do you love him?" It took me a while to figure out the answer. The truth is, I don't think I considered it at all until she asked. I told her, "I think so" and she convinced me that I did. She dared me to call him while we were on the bus to tell him how I felt. I was so nervous but I thought, "Hey, what do I have to lose?" I called him up and Ana was "all ears." As Ray and I spoke over the phone, I blurted out, "I love you." Ana was in the background dancing and I was relieved. Ray? Well he didn't say it back. He was in shock honestly but he did acknowledge my feelings. He wasn't ready for what I was giving him.

Ray and I continued to hangout for a couple of months. It was important for me to be abstinent until I was ready for the next step. We were currently on the six-month mark and I was ready to be with him intimately. It was a choice that happened after he completed a huge favor for me. Weird right? I felt like I had to give him something in return. He showed me how much he cared so it was time to show him how I felt.

We dated for three and a half years. Because of his profession, he was around women all of the time. I will never forget the time we went to a concert in Long Island and his son came with us. We were in the second row enjoying a hip hop show when I noticed Ray started talking to the woman on the opposite side of his seat. The truth is, we are both social butterflies so it didn't faze me until he asked for her number. He did this in front of his son and me. His son looked at me waiting to see what I would do but I was shocked my damn self. Ray said to the woman, "I'll text you the information for the party tomorrow. I hope you can make it." It was then my gut told me who he was but I denied it.

Insecurities started surfacing like the light from a

burning candle. The more women he spoke to, the more insecure I became. We would share a bed, and I would wake up in pain from my hands clutching the sheets from anger. His insecurities grew as well because he knew what he was doing. What was he doing you may ask? Keep reading.

One evening, we went to a celebrity event in Long Island. It was jam packed with people of all ethnicities grinding to the music and having a good time. A few of his friends were hosting the party, so we made our way to the V.I.P. section of the club to sit back, relax, and enjoy the vibe. Within an hour or so, a woman shows up with a group of her friends. She is a well-known manager in the hip-hop industry who started her career in the 90's. She walked in and rolled her eyes at me as if I did something to her. I decided to ignore her because of her entourage, but I soon realized the reason behind her envious behavior.

While Ray and I were having a discussion, she called him over to her table. She didn't acknowledge me or cared about us together at all. The next thing though had me in shock... Ray just got up and went over. He didn't tell her to wait a minute or call her over to us. He dismissed our conversation and galloped his ass over to her within seconds. I was pissed! What made matters worse is that she had the widest smirk I'd ever seen in my life! It was another sign something was going on, but I overshadowed my emotions and continued to stay.

After his mom passed away, things got really bad. He was mean, inconsiderate, and selfish. I always wondered if he acted that way because he didn't mourn his mother's death. I thought he was just tired of being in the relationship. One final argument ended us. Though I was heartbroken, it was the best thing we could have possibly done **for each other.**

CHAPTER FOUR

IT'S TIME TO GO

"I want every day to be a fresh start on expanding what is possible."

-Oprah Winfrey

· · · · · ·  · · · · · ·

It took me a few of months after my initial breakup with Ray to get back into the dating game. My heart was completely broken and I had a lot of baggage. I felt empty and emotionless as I carried on with my days and I put on a major front to my friends. I would play it off like everything was okay and I was pushing through but that breakup torn me apart. Without getting into much detail, our public relationship looked good on the outside. We shared celebrity friends and acquaintances, his family liked me, and we enjoyed each other's company. I would never question if we loved each other but I know now it wasn't pure love. We both definitely held onto the things that would eventually end our relationship. Resentment is a motha. Listening to inspirational music was my only solace. It took almost nine months of recharging my soul to want to date again. His name? Lamont.

Lamont was smart, handsome, and sweet. At that time, he was a teacher and fitness trainer at the New York Sports Club on Court Street in Brooklyn. I'll never forget our first date: we went to a pool hall on Flatbush Avenue. As we gathered the pool sticks and racked the balls for our first round, he said we should make a bet. I was curious and agreed to making a bet on the game. I asked, "What are we betting on?" He said, "If I lose, I have to kiss you, and if you lose, you have to kiss me." I giggled and said, "First base on the first date huh?" He smirked and I said, "Sure, get ready to lose, sucka!"

We flirted the entire first round and I won, but he wasn't having it. He said, "The first person to win three games is the winner." I shook my head and agreed, "Okay, let's do it!" At the end of round two guess who won? Before we started the third round he was nervous to lose: it was quite funny. As we began round three, we lightened things up a bit by asking each other the first date questions like: "What do you do for a living? Where do you live? Are you in school?" As soon as we finished round three and I became the champion, he said, "Bring that face over to me, I am the true winner right now." Me being the Leo that I am, I didn't budge. He looked at me like I was a piece of lemon coconut cake and walked over to me and laid a kiss smack dab on my cheek. He fooled me good too, and we both laughed and made our way to grab a bite to eat.

Over the next four weeks, we went on four dates. When he dropped me off on date number four, he broke the fantasy of fun and was ready for sex. Though I was attracted to him, I thought it was too soon. I didn't want to lead him on so I ended our short-lived relationship. He was pretty pissed off about it too. I could tell he cared for me but I just wasn't ready to get serious with someone so soon.

I lived in Bedford Stuyvesant for four and a half years and it was time to go. I was accepted into Brooklyn College for the winter semester of 2011. I could save money and move from my comfortable one-bedroom apartment into a room by Prospect Park and walk to school. It was the perfect opportunity.

My decision to go back to school was based on my situation at the time. I had been working in marketing and promotions for four years. Though it was not consistent, it paid the bills. While I was working in promotions, I also picked up freelance work as a producer for different corporate companies. Whenever I was hired for those gigs, I always had a feeling of substance and joy. Working as a full-time producer was my goal and I knew that it was time for me to learn what was going on in the entertainment industry.

The time had arrived and it was moving day. I'd been packing the last few items all night with my two friends and taking shots of Patron that was left over in my cabinet. It was easy to persuade them into helping me: free shots of Patron if you help me pack. There they were: Nora the quiet and timid friend hanging with Don the loud and humorous friend. They got along really well. As Don finished the bottle of Patron, light began to appear between the blinds. I looked at the time and it was 5:15 a.m. We needed to wake up in three hours so it was time to get some rest.

I got a text at 9:00 a.m. and my ex-boyfriend Ray was downstairs to pick me up and take me to the rental company. I know, how did he get back in the picture? Honestly, we started to become cordial again. He would start sending random text messages and at first I would ignore them. Then he would become more persistent and I didn't want to hold a grudge so I gave us a chance to be friends again.

While we were on the drive to pick up the rental truck, my feelings were starting to grow fond for him again. It had been over a year from our initial breakup but I couldn't get side tracked, I had to stay focused on the move. Anyhoo, we arrived to the house with the rental truck and there I was with Ray and my two boys from the Bronx, Marvin and

Jason. It was time to go.

We all began to grab boxes. Of course I chose the lighter ones since I had three strong men helping me for the day. After my fourth roundtrip climb to the third floor, I took a break at the truck; the fellas though continued to move. After an hour I headed to the store to buy them breakfast. As we parlayed by the truck, I couldn't control my feelings for Ray. He came out of his way to help me and it was such a turn on that I did the best I could to control myself from kissing him.

"Chop, chop let's get a move on it!" I shouted to the fellas as they all made their way up to the third floor. This time, they were bringing down my beloved bedroom set. I spent a pretty penny for a cherry-wood finished bedroom set from Raymour & Flanigan. First comes the bed frame, then the mattress. The nightstand follows suit as I waited patiently at the truck. My neighbors were passing by with morning greetings and well wishes as my friends continued to grab pieces of furniture from my old apartment. As Ray and Marvin brought down the last piece of furniture from the house, which happened to be a dresser, I ran to the door to keep it ajar. As I was holding the door, Ray gave me a look. It was a look of disappointment and distrust.

All I could think was that he and Marvin must have gotten into an argument upstairs. I let it go until I heard those unforgettable words: *I found your friend in the drawer and I had to close it before Marvin saw it.* I am standing there with three hours of sleep and then BOOM it hit me like a ton of bricks. My heart sank. That gushy feeling I had earlier burst into shattered pieces of embarrassment and shame. I left my dildo in the drawer. Yup I know, get your laughs out now. Did I seriously leave my B.O.B (battery operated boyfriend) in the drawer when I knew three men would be helping me move? To be honest, I didn't know where to pack him! I am serious! I didn't want to put him in any other box besides my own (no pun intended) so I left it there until it

20

was too late. That Patron had me lit and I forgot to handle my business. I grabbed B.O.B from the drawer and shoved it into another box.

After we finished packing and unloading into my new space, I laid on my new bed and laughed out loud so much that my belly ached with splendor! Believe it or not, I haven't used B.O.B since. It felt like someone knew my secret so I could not use him anymore. After that day, we didn't speak to each other for months. He mocked me and made me feel like crap. It was time to go.

The Master's Curse

I was warned back in May of 2011 while applying to school at 26 years old. The deputy chair at Brooklyn College warned me that my life for the next couple of years would be hell. I laughed, she didn't. She warned me that I would be testing my own strength. She also asked me if I had a boyfriend during the interview process, I knew that it was an awkward question. I thought to myself, *What does my no-sex-having-ass have to do with me being accepted into this program?* She explained that it was easier to complete the program as a single woman. Well checkmate because I was already living the single life.

The deputy chair had been working there for over ten years and she knew what she was talking about or at least it felt that way at the moment. Only a small group of people was accepted into the program and there was a twenty to thirty percent dropout rate. This dropout rate was based on the completion of the first semester. There are two things I quit in my life: an AP English class in high school that required me to read five long form books in one month and working in an after school program at 15 years old. That percentage rate did not scare me since I knew that completing my Master's was a dream opportunity. I took her advice in stride but never could I imagine how accurate she was. I was missing a big part in my college life: intimacy.

A new problem surfaced: I realized throughout my first semester of college I was losing friends. I had a tendency to love hard. This includes friendships and relationships alike, so it hurt me to the core that some people that I trusted and adored exited my life with no explanation. I then started creating stories of the breakups. These stories went something like, "Oh I knew she was always jealous of me, I am there for her more than she is there for me anyway so she can go to hell!" I admire and love my friends but when they stopped reaching out to me, I would cut them off (this has been my defense mechanism since I was a little girl.) I rarely had any family around (extra-small family) so I always took things personal when people did not show up in my life. All I could think about was my feelings but I never considered what their experiences were of me.

Mid-semester, which happened to fall in October, I realized I was forming another habit. It wasn't a habit that I was very proud of, but it was a habit that carried me along the way. Alcohol. Prior to being with my ex Ray, I was a social drinker. While we were together, we would drink almost every night. That habit changed from being a social drinker to being more dependent. He would use it to help with his sleep disorder after working long hours at night, and I was drinking only because he was drinking. Knowing this now, I know how unhealthy this unforeseen habit was and how it continued to grow.

We went from drinking a pint of vodka to completing a fifth each night. When we would spend time together on the weekends, I was throwing away at least two vodka bottles every weekend. The funny thing is, I would only drink this way when we were together. Throughout the week, I may have a drink here and there but not every day. This started up a feeling of neglect in me as a prior ex depended on smoking weed. *Why did I attract these types of men? What form of intimacy was I attracting into my life that was invalid?* It was the perfect time for me to evaluate myself and find out.

I was currently enrolled in one of the toughest graduate programs and I had no one to share it with. I never felt so alone in my life. I was starting to suffer from depression. I would be tipsy, editing a project up until four in the morning, which would be due the same day at 10 a.m.! It was starting to take control of my life. And this time I officially started to believe I was falling into a trap. *How could I, Bernice Wooden, let myself spiral into this web*? It is one of the hardest things I had to admit to myself. I never told a soul and I was embarrassed.

But why?

So here is the million-dollar question: Why are you celibate, Bernice? The three main reasons people choose to be celibate include the following: religious reasons, self-discovery, and heartbreaks. There are a couple of factors to my celibacy. First, I decided after breaking up with Ray that I would not have sex until I figured out a few things about myself. It was one of those things where they say, "You are giving your milk away for free," and I grew tired of relationships where the sex was good and the friendships were fun but nothing else seemed to develop. Second, I feared getting pregnant and not being married. Having children without marriage is common in my DNA so I want to be the shift in my family. Third, it was time to really get to know me. Know my likes, dislikes, loves, and everything in between. I knew it would be hard for anyone to love me if I'm uncertain or unsure of myself. I was so used to loving people with restrictions that it was time for a change.

It's truly eye opening to see where I have been blocked in my previous friendships and relationships. I can honestly admit that I never loved anyone unconditionally besides my mother. Because my family is super small and we all live in different parts of the country, it was always hard for me to understand the definition of "family." I knew what it was and everyone else in my life had it, but I never felt it and for this reason I felt lonely.

Through my loneliness, I gravitated to the idea of wanting a soul mate. I want someone who will love and honor all of my strengths and flaws. Someone who will capture the essence of my love by just... being. It took me over three years to really pinpoint what I want in life and in a relationship so I've compiled a list that supported me.

These seven things keep me grounded and centered:

1. Learning how to love myself flaws and all through discovery.

2. Creating a new standard of self-worth.

3. Channeling my energy towards other purposes.

4. Strengthening those purposes and deciding not to lead with my sexuality.

5. Being open to true love.

6. Discovering the highest meaning of intimacy.

7. Protecting my mind and body from negative energy.

You're 30, now what?

When I turned 30 years old, I decided to spend my birthday week in Los Angeles. The morning of my birthday, as I was sleeping on my friend's couch, I began crying my eyeballs out at how empty I felt. A milestone birthday in L.A. turned into a solo pity party. I allowed the critiques in my mind to take over my body and I was sad for most of the day. All I could think about was being a single woman with no career and no family. It took a toll on me but things quickly shifted when I shared my feelings with a friend on the phone.

She reminded me that my patience was being tested, and I needed to go through the process. At first I wasn't trying to hear it, but then I opened up to what the possibilities were if I listened. It was then that I decided that I would have control over my emotions and body. It felt good to release my negative emotions and move through the rest of the trip being inspired and empowered. I was happy again. You cannot be happy with someone else if you are not happy by yourself.

In this book, I will discuss my top ten steps to celibacy that continue to create a fulfilling experience. It is important to note that there are many ways to being empowered through celibacy however the tools I choose to cover are ones I follow on a daily basis and they have created the most clarity for me. I am excited to share what inspires me for a healthy, loving and fun relationship with myself.

Part II: THE WORK

CHAPTER FIVE

STEP ONE

CAN YOU KEEP A SECRET?

"I feel bare, I didn't realize I wore my secrets as armor until they were gone and now everyone sees me as I really am."

-Veronica Roth

G rad school was rough. I lost two best friends due to my stubborn ways. I was working part-time at Brooklyn College as a college assistant, and I was picking up promotional gigs on the weekends while I was completing school assignments. Though I chose this patch of uncertainty (grad school and celibacy), I never realized that I would have to do it in solitude. At the time, none of my friends were on the same journey as me so some relationships felt strained. They would share less with me because they thought it would make me feel uncomfortable knowing I wasn't "getting any." It was one of the hardest things I've ever decided to do. My mother was becoming distant because I wasn't around, and things were starting to fall apart. It was a place that I never care to go again.

I had to re-route my journey and really begin looking at my life through a magnifying glass. *Why are you choosing to go through this journey alone? What support is available when you need it? How will you grow from this experience?* I slowly began to answer these questions to figure out what this journey would mean to me. Once I dug deep and figured it all out, I knew my secret had to remain just that... a secret.

The first year of celibacy was the hardest because I was constantly thinking about sex and whether I had started my journey with the wrong intentions. While listening to other people's stories about breakups, I noticed people found comfort in learning about themselves while others had fun with rebounds. Negative thoughts started filling my mind: *I am young, vibrant and beautiful- why would I restrict myself? Sex is natural and needed, why do this now?* These were my thoughts and it would run havoc on my mind every day. I soon became envious of loving relationships and wondered if I would ever have someone love me the same way. *What was I doing differently? Why was it so hard to love myself through this process?*

I've had people in my life who said, "Oh, I need sex. How can you go without it? You're in your twenties, you're missing out. You're too young to do something like that. Why would you deprive yourself from having sex? Why would you do that to yourself?" And then I have others who are in their thirties and forties who said, "Honey, you're doing the right thing. You think you had the best sex of your life so far, but you haven't. There's more to come. You are still learning your body so don't feel pressured to do anything you don't want to do." Just a small group of friends asked about my journey and genuinely were interested in my reasons. You have to shield your heart and accept the positive reinforcements and dismiss the negative influences. Oh and let's not forget the person who made me feel guilty about what I was doing to MY body. I broke off our friendship with the quickness.

After I completed my first year of celibacy, I sent a text message out to my friends to give them the news and they replied with comments like, "You got this! Go for more! You go girl!" One friend even said, "You should go for five years!" I replied to him and said, "Oh hell no! Why would I do that?" It felt good to be acknowledged for my efforts and thought: *Hey maybe another year wouldn't hurt.*

While I reserved some parts of my life to new friends and acquaintances, my conversations with old friends started to feel more loving and complete over time. They didn't pressure me to change or be anything other than myself. They started realizing that I was serious and I meant business. I was finally ready to hear their stories about their relationships without it feeling like a homework assignment. When I let go of the notion that I was not alone, my friends poured love into me more than I could ever imagine. Sex and intimacy was starting to appear in my life in other ways.

People that I adored and admired would openly share their intimate stories with me and it was the first time during this journey that I was open to living vicariously through them with no vengeance in my heart. As I shared earlier, I use to listen to my friends in high school share their stories and I would live vicariously through them but this was different. At that time, I didn't have sex so of course the imagination can only lead to what you think you know. What shifted now is that I've had sexual experiences and now I was open to exploring my friend's intimate rendezvous without judgment and with joy. I have always been the friend people pour into. *I am the secret keeper but who would hold my secret?*

My friendships during celibacy continue to be best supported by those who can love me fully and pour positive energy into my life. Those who maintain integrity keep me balanced. I personally have found encouragement with sharing goals and outcomes that have kept my friends intrigued by my courage, and have them pondering the notion to join in on the fun.

Now don't get me wrong, there are a few challenges I've faced early on this journey. Here is a list of downer's:

- Weight gain

- Depression

- Being Quick-tempered

- Uncertainty

First, weight gain has been a struggle for me since I was a child. My weight would "yo-yo" every two years since I was 12 years old. It would be a constant struggle with 30 pounds. I would say it's one of the things that Janet Jackson and I have in common. I usually gain weight in two stages of my life: when I'm sad/upset or when I stop going to the gym.

Second, depression oh how you slide into my life! I never thought I would be depressed but it is more common in the world than I thought. Depression is one of the most unsettling feelings I've ever felt because most times it comes out of nowhere. I just want to crawl up in a ball and listen to sad R&B songs all day and of course binge eat.

Third, I have been a quick-tempered firecracker since I was a little girl. It has been a defense mechanism that has both supported me and debilitated me. I share this candidly because it is something I still struggle with. It is a trait that I have learned from my mother and I want to change it sooner than later.

Last but not least, uncertainty drives me insane and it has kept me stuck in more ways than one. I may not try something new because I automatically think I will fail or

I cannot do it. It is another trait I saw in my household and that's why my secrets mean more to me than anything else.

Even though I have struggled with these "downer's" during my journey, they have painted a clear picture for me to change my life tremendously. What kind of cycle would I continue if I were to face these struggles in a relationship? Things surely wouldn't change but now that I am vocal about them, I can work towards eliminating them one step at a time.

Also during my first year of celibacy, I started transformational work in the heart of Midtown. The workshops helped me get to the point of knowing that I had to let go and let God guide me on this journey we call life.

July 4th 2011 is the last time I had sex and during the first year of celibacy, I continued to paint sexual images in my mind. My body could still feel the touch of my last partner and I remember vividly how I felt at climax. I began to question the sanity of my decision and I started to convince myself that this was a BIG FAT MISTAKE. I was thinking about my ex but for all of the wrong reasons.

When I initially decided to become celibate, I wasn't sure how long I should abstain from sex. I then also had to figure out the difference between being celibate and abstinent. For those of you who are still unsure, abstinence is having no sexual indulgence. Some reasons behind abstaining from sex may include: no sexual desire, being pregnant, being "too busy" for sex and more. Celibacy on the other hand is a choice that comes from within, and is made to achieve a goal. Though the definitions can be used simultaneously, I find more strength in using the word celibacy. My closest friends know the process I've been going through. I was once set on the idea of waiting until my next relationship but I've recently upgraded that definition to waiting until marriage. I know how important it is to stand for something that you truly believe in and I want to create a loving relationship without sex. Intimacy will be my primary goal in my future relationship.

After learning the true definition, I decided whatever I was going to do I would be in control. Why did I want control? Well I didn't have it in my previous relationship. I thought I was supposed to make my boyfriend happy by any means necessary. Sex was something I thought I had to do to keep him happy. Though he seemed happy, I surely wasn't. It was hard to be in a relationship with Ray when I gave him my all.

I've had so many people ask me, *How long should someone abstain from sex?* Well first let me preface this question. Clearly everyone's situation is different. I believe it is important to know your intention before you decide how long it should be. I will also add that your intention should come from within as many times we may make calculated decisions because we are upset or angry. If you are solid with your intention and understand the importance of your decision than I will suggest that it is important to abstain from sex for at least one year... yes one full year.

Imagine 365 days of being with you and the new things you will learn about yourself. Not only do you want to break a habit, but you want to start new habits that will support your new decision and build a foundation. It is actually one of the smartest things I have ever done! My confidence level is higher than before, I have more time to be of service and build my spiritual relationship with the universe and God. Being with yourself is also more about creating positive mental wellness and spirituality in manifesting things for your future that you never thought were imaginable.

As you continue to choose who will know your journey, create a space of honesty and vulnerability. They too may be considering the same process and the both of you can support each other. Celibacy has made me a more positive person. It has shown me humility and it continues to keep me in tune with my body. It made me grow spiritually and mentally. It has helped me break boundaries that I set up for myself that I thought I couldn't do, especially with getting my graduate degree and completing it within two years.

The key is to never share your personal journey with someone who will ridicule you and make fun of you or try to convince you to give up on your goal. Finding yourself is nothing to laugh or joke about. Stay far away from those that question your sanity and question your reasons. Everyone's journey is not the same and you should not feel disempowered because someone made you feel bad.

I give in abundance all of the time so just imagine what life is like always giving and not receiving. I did learn however by giving too much, I am incapable of loving completely so I made a promise to myself that I would love myself first before anyone comes into my life. I also made a promise that my next relationship would be filled with authenticity and love, I will never settle for less.

What defines who I am is defined by me and me only. Rhonda Bryne author of *Big Magic* shares, "Whether you have been aware of your thoughts in the past or not, now you are becoming aware." And for me, I didn't know how vital my actions were in my past relationships until I sat with myself and marinated in my stillness.

Exercise #1: List the top 3 people in your life who will lovingly accept your celibacy journey and what do you think the conversation will sound like. If you do plan to share this information with each of them, how will it make you feel? Would you be scared or feel free? Write down your thoughts below.

• • • • 💋 • • • •

_____

_____

_____

_____

_____

_____

_____

_____

_____

_____

_____

_____

_____

_____

_____

_____

_____

CHAPTER SIX

STEP TWO

MASSAGE IT

"I just want mind-boggling sex tonight, but I don't think you can beat my vibrator."

-Anna Bayes

Now before we move further, how often do you connect with your body? Connection can be many things. For one, how often do you admire your body in the mirror while being naked? Or when was the last time you massaged lotion into your skin with passion, ease, and sensuality? Another truth that has supported me through celibacy is truly owning who you are and learning every nook and cranny of your body. From your sweet spots to the fluffy spots all have meaning. What most people don't realize is that you can still be intimate without having a partner in your life. What does that look like exactly? Well in this chapter I will discuss self-pleasure.

Is it true that I think about sex every day? Well yes, yes I do. How often do you ask? Well, I have no idea, but I can say that I take almost everything out of context. Let me give you an example: if someone says, "OMG, he's cute!" My "cute detector" either agrees or disagrees. If my detector disagrees, my imagination is free from foreplay and hardcore sex; if he is cute better yet if he is fione (an exaggerated expression of fine: looking good) my mind whirls into a euphoria of hot, steamy, bed-rocking, earth-shattering, and mind-blowing intercourse. That imagination of mine can cause friction and it can be a distraction sometimes but that is where my journey takes me. Where does your mind take you?

Though sex is more freely spoken about in television shows and film, self-pleasure is still considered a taboo subject. Finding pleasure with one's self is one of the most important steps in this celibacy journey. Though I choose not to be in a relationship and not have sex, I do find pleasure in pleasing myself. Self-pleasure is beneficial because it releases stress, tension, and discomfort, and it just makes you feel good (for more details about the importance of self-pleasure, please conduct your own research.) While I may not "release" myself every day, sometimes things can trigger an emotion, and I know it's time to get down to business. There are different tools like: self-penetration, clitoral stimulation, toys, or the right jeans! I actually know a few women who shared with me that they would walk around "commando" to please themselves throughout the day without placing their fingers anywhere near their pussies.

What I learned most about being single and being a woman who pleases herself, it is important to be in tune with your body. In my previous relationships, I was quite insecure and hated to have sex with the lights on. I mean how many women love that? If you do, boo! LOL. Whenever the lights were on, I never really enjoyed the sexual experience, I would just hope that my partner would release sooner than later so I can get under the covers. How do you become secure in your body when you fear looking at yourself in the mirror or exploring your temple?

Usually after I share that I am celibate with someone, the next question they usually ask is if I use self-pleasure for stimulation. I am always honest with this question and shout from the mountaintops a high YES! One thing is for sure, during my sexually active years, talking about sex and masturbation made me blush like a red apple, and I would shy away from sharing my experiences. Now that I am secure with who I am and what I have become, these conversations do not bother me one bit. You know they say, "The older you get, the less fucks you give." Now don't get me wrong, not every single person in my life knows about the importance of self-pleasure but I am pleased to announce that it is one decision I stand by.

Here is the thing about self-pleasure: you do not have to share this part of your journey with people. It is solely up to you what you want to share. I believe that being candid inspires people to be their best even if they are not on the same path as you. *Who will I be when I start being intimate again?* Well I know for sure I will be stronger and more open to trying new things like having sex with the lights on! Self-love has also been a wakeup call for me. I realize that my imagination is fueled by my dreams.

How many times have you released some built up tension to the sounds of some R&B crooner filling up the walls in your bedroom, living room or bathtub? It goes a little something like this: you are listening to some sexy tunes blasting on your home entertainment system or maybe even your phone and you are sipping some full-bodied red wine. You close your eyes and start bopping to the music and all of a sudden you start feeling warm and tingly inside. You then gently caress your skin like it's new territory all the while imagining it's someone else's touch. You then ease your hands into your panties and whoa! Euphoria kicks in, fireworks begin to spark and your body starts to tremor. All of a sudden you jerk left, right, up and down only to hold back from exploding into another galaxy. Once you release, you open your eyes, and smile gently like the world patiently waited for your new soul. Being in tune with your body is powerful.

I do want to point out that we all know that self-pleasure is not a replacement for sex but it carries you through the journey with ease. For those who decide not to use self-pleasure as a form of intimacy, I would consider following all the other steps in this book and do what makes you happy. It's very important to stay connected to your sexuality. If that means taking pole or dance classes that focus on clearing your root chakra, be open to connection and being sensual.

Speaking about sensuality, it doesn't matter if you're doing it for three months, three years, or ten years, you must have boundaries with yourself. Figure out what those boundaries are for you. Are you currently in a relationship and you don't want to have sex until marriage? Are you okay with kissing your partner and sticking to first base? Does your partner accept your journey and is he or she supportive? Have you both agreed to fondling each other or just cuddling? As a quick reminder from chapter two, what makes your journey stress-free is based on the people you share your experience with. I personally have decided that kissing is my "drink of choice" and I have been doing well since July 4, 2010 (my last sexual experience.)

If you have any questions about self-pleasure, talk candidly to your doctor. Also foods like oysters, chocolate, asparagus and watermelon are well-known natural aphrodisiacs. Eating any of those foods can help boost your experience. Your doctors have heard it all before so don't be shy. Though difficult to discuss, self-pleasure is a common conversation for doctors because we know they do it too! Research blog articles and see what show's up for you. Remember, not everyone is alike. Be open to reading as much as possible so you don't feel like you are alone. Also, if you are unsure about stimulation, check out some videos online. You may also consider watching soft porn to learn a few tricks.

Fall in love with your body and keep the lights on.

Exercise #2: Write down what forms of stimulation will keep you grounded through your celibacy journey. Also write down your *no no's* when it comes to having a partner in your life. What is it that you both agree on that will replace intercourse? Make sure you and your partner are clear.

· · · · 💋 · · · ·

_____

_____

_____

_____

_____

_____

_____

_____

_____

_____

_____

_____

_____

_____

_____

_____

CHAPTER SEVEN

STEP THREE

HUG THEN REPEAT!

"I have learned that there is more power in a good strong hug than in a thousand meaningful words."

-Ann Hood

Now for me, although I have been celibate for seven years, I see that I do still need a man's touch. That includes and is not limited to: flirting, sitting next to each other with our arms or legs touching, and the one I love most: HUGS! It is so important to be around the energy of a man through this process. Though it may not be easy when you first consider what you are asking your body to do, but you have to be patient. You have to learn how to control your body. For me, I sit down and think each and everyday, *Okay, you're still human Bernice, and you still need some form of affection, even though you are not doing any sexual activities*. Just a quick touch of someone's hand through a handshake can shift energy and space.

Hugs for me are the most genuine, thoughtful, and respectful way of keeping your goal in check. Hugs from men are always my favorite form of intimacy and that is all I need through my experience. Depending on the man, I may think of them sexually after the hug or I may not. It also depends on our relationship as well. A lot of the men in my life are people I respect and value and they know a lot about my experiences. These men have actually been more supportive than the women I know. Weird right? My male friends usually say, "Bernice, keep it going! The man you are looking for is coming soon" and I also hear, "Bernice, you are such a brave woman to choose celibacy at your age." To best honest, they are right. How many 20 year olds decided to be celibate after having sexual experiences?

I consider myself Dr. Hug! I can hug someone and feel their energy right away. Hugs have pulled me through my lightest and darkest times and I don't know how people offer them being inauthentic. I rather someone say, "I'm not a hugger" than to receive a hug that has no value or was forced. Any form of energy swapping can build walls or build love.

Saying no has also been a powerful tool through this journey. The "no's" to the men who cat call on the street and to the women who try to shame me during this process have become second nature to me. My intuition grows tremendously through this process and I began to trust myself more than ever. I take those "fake hugs" and I want to shove them back in their faces.

The *Merriam-Webster Dictionary* defines a hug: to press tightly especially in the arms. I will also add that it's pressure and energy amongst two or more bodies. That's a genuine hug. I'm not talking about just receiving a hug from a guy you're interested in and want to date. I mean, a genuine hug that can make your day brighter and make your soul lighter.

While I was in graduate school, the genuine hugs kept me aligned and ready to tackle the world! I don't know what would happen if I didn't embrace awesome people while in college. I was alone most of the time and all I could think about was drinking. It was a sad situation to be in but I learned through my breakdowns how powerful my breakthroughs would be. Those same breakthroughs gave me the courage to write this book.

Just knowing how to manage my personal space efficiently and having balance have lead me to the path that I want to be. For example, with riding the trains in New York City every day I have to factor in personal space and be observant to energies present around me. When I sense negative energy, I usually move to another subway car because I don't want the negativity to bounce on me. It's as easy as me watching someone being negative and thinking to myself: *What is his or her problem? Let me love because their negativity can bounce on me and screw up my entire day!*

Protect your energy and space like it's priceless.

Exercise #3: What forms of *energy swapping* would help you stay on the course of your journey? Would hugs be all you need or is cuddling an option? Figure out the touch and energy that will push you forward.

· · · · 💋 · · · ·

_____

_____

_____

_____

_____

_____

_____

_____

_____

_____

_____

_____

_____

_____

_____

_____

_____

CHAPTER EIGHT

STEP FOUR

PAMPER YOURSELF

"Self-care is not selfish. You cannot serve from an empty vessel."

-Elenor Brownn

· · · · · ·  · · · · · · ·

Pampering yourself is one of the major keys to getting in tune with your body and being celibate. You form new habits that keep you grounded and feeling good. Now consider this when was the last time you really enjoyed your own company? How did you feel being alone? Were you sad and depressed or finally happy to decompress? If you do not love yourself when you are alone, then you wouldn't love yourself when you are with someone else. Pampering allows your body to be at ease and feel pure bliss. For one, I love booking spa sessions for my friends and me. We can sit in a Jacuzzi, sip on some champagne, talk, and cackle like little girls as we reminisce. I also enjoy taking myself to the movies and meeting people in the theater. Usually when the movie is over and I am walking out with the crowd, I may ask someone how they enjoyed the film and would they recommend it to a friend.

51

I love to engage with others especially when I am feeling good. There are so many ways you can pamper yourself. You can read a book at the park, get a manicure and pedicure, treat yourself to a concert and dance the night away! What I love most about trying new things through the pamper process, is that I continue to learn the things that I like and dislike. I feed from the activities that allow me to be my best self.

For many of us, it takes this personal journey to push us through what makes us happy. While I mention some materialistic things, the most important pampering I enjoy is transformational work. I have been investing in my body and mind for the past seven years. I have attended workshops and courses that have improved my well-being. I decided to live in the now and give my mind all of my attention. Consider expanding your definition of pampering to self-love and care for the mind with groups and organizations that can elevate you.

The two art forms that I find to be most therapeutic are dancing and painting. I love dance classes that allow you to just move whichever way your body is called to move. Imagine how much bravery and courage you have to be in a room full of strangers to sway your hips and let go? It's also the same with painting. Using a brush to stroke a canvas or object is so sensual to me. I love how much power we have in our wrists. I feel like they are the "mastermind" of our hands. Depending on the setting both dancing and painting can be intimate art forms that can connect you with your body. I enjoy dancing in a dim light to soft music with a heavy base. We all have our preferences.

For those who love to look good, how about treating yourself to a new lipstick brand and color? I usually do this once a month. I would buy my new lipstick and wear it religiously for a week! I then find other tools in my makeup kit that make me feel beautiful as I try new colors and palettes.

After you've taken care of some of those pamper trips and new experiences, how do you feel? How are you shifting in your life to enjoy your alone time and being present with yourself? Don't you feel lighter knowing that you can focus on you and only you?

Think of one thing you can do for yourself on a daily basis. Consider your alone time a part of your schedule and mark it in your planner. My alone time starts at the top of the morning with a ten to twenty-minute meditation, writing in my journal, burning some sage and putting oils on my hands. I leave the house ready to start a new day. Whenever I miss my morning routine, I feel incomplete and groggy. Start a morning routine that works for you. If that means waking up thirty minutes earlier so you can feel good throughout the day then do it! **It's for YOU!**

Stay in tune with all aspects of your femininity. You know how you feel when you get your hair curled or purchase a new summer dress? You can't wait to show it off! While I was in graduate school, it was important for me to get my hair and nails done bi-weekly. When that masculine touch is not available (by choice of course) you still want to feel desired.

Everyone believes in different forms of pampering so don't feel confined to the things you read here. Explore what pampering means to you.

Exercise #4: What activities will make you feel good that will keep you moving through this journey and feeling confident? List some of your favorite activities here and be open to doing these activities with yourself or with friends.

· · · · 💋 · · · ·

_____

_____

_____

_____

_____

_____

_____

_____

_____

_____

_____

_____

_____

_____

_____

_____

_____

CHAPTER NINE

STEP FIVE

LET'S DATE!

"I think part of being an adult is leaving the fairytale behind."

-Rashida Jones

Dating is one of the most important times in anyone's life. It is a time of networking, connection, and fun! Why would I restrict myself to all of the juiciness on the planet because I'm taking some time to connect to my soul? As you can see through the steps so far in this book, I don't have to move through this journey bored, lonely and tired! I can be a powerful woman who leads life with confidence and be clear on my needs and wants.

Dating is a very important element in the celibacy journey because the scene changes frequently. Certain treads stay current like: online dating and meeting through a mutual friend. Oh and let's not forget the casual conversations at an outing but what about the "new wave" of dating? Things have shifted so much! Instead of phone conversations, people usually rely on text messaging. I retracted from dating and continued my journey alone because of the expectation of text dating. I was stuck. It was

like living in a recurring nightmare. I would have a date and then we would continue the conversation through text...
BORING!

When I first started thinking about celibacy I didn't want to date. I thought it would be a distraction to accomplishing my goals. For the first two years I didn't date and it was painful. I felt ugly and unwanted. I think it is another reason why I depended on alcohol. I also held back from dating because I thought men needed to know about my celibacy right away. While exploring and finally dating, I've noticed that conversations about sex on the first date is a buzz kill (unless sex naturally is brought up in the conversation.) For most of the dates I've been on, we may discuss sex on the third or fourth date and when that happens, I candidly share my story. Many times they don't call back and guess what? That's okay too.

I have dated men who have not expected anything from me, as I didn't from them. Dating is one of those tools if, "you don't use it, you lose it." Though the dating process may seem tiresome and time-consuming, consider how many dates you want to have per month. For me, I would consider at least one date bi-weekly to be ideal. New Yorkers I have a disclaimer: I get it. Some of us have to work over forty hours a week to pay the bills, work tirelessly at two jobs and be an entrepreneur. We are going on "less dates" because we need to keep a roof over our heads and that is the focus for most of us but listen: don't lose your mojo. The scary part is that it can happen so quickly. Two years away from the dating scene had me terrified.

Now that I am dating more frequently, I am always clear when it comes to the date setting. The best dates I've ever been on were doing things like: walking in the park, grabbing a tan on the beach or just grabbing a drink at the bar.

Not everyone is set up for dating. It all depends on what you choose to do. If dating is not the plan for your personal goals, schedule weekly fun dates with friends to keep you in the know about dating and listen to their stories. Some of the things my friends share with me are way more advanced than the things I've experienced. Stories of BDSM, orgies, and other sexual experiences filled up my ears over cocktails, but I will say I love hearing about their sexual experiences. It not only entertains me but it makes me happy to see that my friends are happy.

Consider what your dating experiences would be like if you were open to meeting people during your celibacy journey. You never know what it can lead to. Though dating was rough throughout my graduate school experience due to numerous tedious college assignments, I have built stronger relationships with the opposite sex due to being open. I have always enjoyed hearing from different men about their perspective on life. I can feel protected and loved by my best friend who just happens to be a man and there goes my win/win. *How can you strengthen your relationships with the opposite sex to gain clarity about your choices?* Be mindful to the process and just trust.

I'll never forget the morning I woke up and said, *All right, God. Now I'm ready for a man to come into my life. It has been four years of building myself and I want to be touched and loved by someone.* But then again I said, *All right. How true is that? Do I want a fling? Do I want a one-night stand? Or do I really want to commit to being with someone?* Insecurity started to set in and the market for single men seemed slim to none. So in 2014, the summer came and I hadn't gone on one date. I couldn't believe that I'd attended social events almost every day and felt like I was back to square one. I was starting to question my femininity. I would have questions like, *Why is this dating thing so hard? What vibes am I releasing? Is it true that I really want a relationship?*

Then the simplest thing dawned on me: *Bernice, you declared that you would not get into a relationship until THIS book was complete so you can authentically be celibate when the book releases.* It's truly amazing how powerful our words are and what impact they have on our day-to-day lives. It was a constant reminder that: I too can declare something and my words have meaning.

After saying that prayer and seeing it evolve into fruition, I had to cope with what would happen next. Now in the summer I saw gorgeous, shirtless men ALL THE TIME. Men who walked around chiseled, dripping sweat, and just being in their greatness. They are so beautiful that I would say to myself, *Okay. I need one of those now* and then I would get a gentle reminder from above like, *Hey Bernice, it ain't happening, remember what you said?*

When I tell you that entire spring semester in 2014 was hard, it was hard. I was used to being flattered and smiling to funny pick-up lines but everything changed after I said that prayer. I should have said, *Lord I want the attention from men but I don't want to date them.* Now that I think about it, I would probably be considered a tease but at that time, it didn't matter. It was becoming difficult for me to cope with so I was ready for a relationship or at least I thought so.

For those who are in a relationship right now and you want to build your relationship into celibacy, write down a list of the pros and cons of being celibate during the relationship and read your list to each other to see if it will be valuable. It is important to note that this will create a new foundation for your relationship. Are you up for the challenge?

I am going to say the next statement in CAPS: YOU DO NOT WANT TO FEEL PRESSURED OR PERSUADED TO DO ANYTHING THAT YOU DON'T WANT TO DO. Be clear with your intentions while dating and everything that needs to be shared on your date while being authentic and loving. Being clear about your reason for being celibate will not only prove maturity and trust in the relationship, but it will lead to a better understanding of what you are trying to do in your life. Hopefully you meet someone who will understand, and if not, then you know what you have to do.

Another factor I had to dig deep into was my problem of putting others before me. It was something that I have done ever since I was a young child. For me it was a form of feeling wanted and needed. When I entered into adulthood and did the same thing in my romantic relationships, I of course, would get the short end of the stick and who wants that? When I realized that was something I was doing to myself, it secured me in believing that I needed time apart from everyone and really sit down and figure out the W's:

1.Who am I?

2. Why am I here?

3. What am I doing to get me where I want to go?

4. Where will I be if I decided not to change?

5. When am I ready for the transition to begin?

I had to create a space of love and healing so that when it's time to date again, I won't feel awkward. I don't want it to feel like it's my first time all over again. I want to provide gratitude, love, joy, and abundance.

I've learned: when I grown and find out who I really am, I can give more because I know more. You know what they say, "The more you give the more you receive." Create a mentality that the more you learn about yourself the more you can teach others how to treat you, especially while dating.

Two-Part Exercise: Exercise #5A: Write down the answers to the following questions shared in this chapter: Who am I? Why am I here? What am I doing to get me where I want to go? Where will I be if I decided not to change? When am I ready for the transitioning to begin?

· · · · 👄 · · · ·

_____

_____

_____

_____

_____

_____

_____

_____

_____

_____

_____

_____

_____

_____

_____

_____

_____

Exercise #5B: Now that you are clear about the 5 W's, write down the perfect date that doesn't include sex. What would you discuss and how would the date play out for the evening.

· · · · 💋 · · · ·

_____

_____

_____

_____

_____

_____

_____

_____

_____

_____

_____

_____

_____

_____

_____

_____

_____

CHAPTER TEN

STEP SIX

IN TO ME YOU SEE

"Be willing to share all of who you are. So many of us want a partner, but we're not willing to show all of us."

-Iyanla Vanzant

One of my favorite motivational speakers, Melvin Britton-Miller shared his definition of intimacy in one of his workshops. He defined Intimacy as, "In- To- Me-You-See." It is one of the most powerful definitions I've ever heard and I use it as a staple for all of my relationships.

As I add to Mr. Britton-Miller's definition, I will also say that intimacy is two people together, sharing with each other, holding hands, and loving on each other. As I mentioned before, what I did notice most about my early start on this journey was I lacked intimacy. I wasn't dating or spending time with friends, I was pretty much living in a sheltered state of being. I was putting myself on such a lockdown that I didn't even know what was going on in the world at that time. I skipped out on news reports (other than updates from people's social media accounts) and I was focused on getting my degree. School was my focus and nothing else.

My New Year's resolution during my second year of celibacy was something along the lines of praying that I can hold my celibacy for another year. *You know God, if anything happens in regards to men coming into my life, I fully accept that. However, it's going to be on my terms.* And at that time, my terms were I'm not going to have sex until I was ready.

I always believed that women should not be calculated by the amount of sex they've had in life. Being a woman is complicated more times than ever so learning what femininity and womanhood means will make your experience more successful.

It took me almost six years to define what intimacy means to me. It is the personal experience you have with every person on the planet. It is not just marked by romantic relationships, it allows you to love and be loved…freely.

Exercise #6: Now that you have a different perspective about intimacy, what are you learning about yourself and are you holding back from someone else because he or she lacks connection and intimacy? Write down ways you can be intimate without having sex.

• • • • 💋 • • • •

_____

_____

_____

_____

_____

_____

_____

_____

_____

_____

_____

_____

_____

_____

_____

_____

CHAPTER ELEVEN

STEP SEVEN

GOALS AND CAREER MINDSET

"Be passionate and move forward with gusto every single hour of every single day until you reach your goal."

-Ava DuVernay

How many times have you heard athletes abstaining from sex before a professional game? It is no rumor how sex can support the mind, body, and spirit, but many times it can be a distraction from the goals you want to attain. Keep your game face on and tackle your goals like it is the last thing for you to do on the planet! Sex is great and success is great too. You ABSOLUTELY can have both! Remember though, it takes time and ease to learn how to balance the two.

Working in the entertainment industry has taught me that you must have more than one skill. My dream is to become a successful entrepreneur, I knew I had to know a little bit of everything so I learned how to produce and direct as well. However, I was only attracting editing work.

Because this was my least favorite thing to do at that time, I thought there was only one way I could get through it which incorporated alcohol. When I was freelancing and there was an editing job that could cover my rent for a couple of months, why would I want to turn that down?

As I started my first semester, I had a music video due within the first three weeks. After aligning my talent, production, it was time for me to edit. My ritual for a weekend of editing was something like: liquor store, liquor store, and more liquor store. I would start editing at 6 p.m. and finish around 2 a.m. For me, I was most comfortable editing at night and the guilt of drinking didn't seem so bad since my roommates were not around at the time. I felt no one was around to judge me. Monday morning included one empty bottle of rum and a sore ass from editing all weekend. Life was grand (enter sarcasm here).

I then sat down and realized the game I was playing with my life. How can I be a well sought out entrepreneur and reach my career goals having the fear of being great? I have struggled a long time with the fear of success. It is actually very paralyzing and hard to deal with. For me, I love learning and education but when asked to do something outside of my comfort zone, I freeze and feel stuck. How many times in life were you presented with something outside your comfort zone and ended up feeling stuck?

Women are independent now more than ever. We like to do things for ourselves, and we are more career-focused than previous years. Back in the day a woman was expected to be a wife, homemaker, crochet, and be satisfied doing these things. Well life is quite different these days. A lot of women aspire to do these things and more. Being successful has become very important for so many women in order to achieve fulfillment.

I believe one major challenge of being a career woman is

the pressure of being in a relationship or having sex while in one because it is the norm. It is me that should define what I want in my life. Building a successful career involves making serious, sometimes difficult decisions and I knew this time around, I had to stay focused.

Set the tone to focus on your career to reach your desired goals. If you are not satisfied with your career, it is easier to "change lanes" without the pressure from a partner. Also stir clear from comparing your experiences to other people in your life. If you want to win the game in your career, set goals and stretch but keep your integrity. The independent woman CANNOT do it all alone, but it is fine to slow down to slay personal goals.

Exercise #7: What career goals/everyday goals would you be able to achieve if sex wasn't in the picture? Write down goals that you've been holding back on achieving and what steps it will take to complete them.

· · · · 💋 · · · ·

_____

_____

_____

_____

_____

_____

_____

_____

_____

_____

_____

_____

_____

_____

_____

_____

CHAPTER TWELVE

STEP EIGHT

MEDITATION

"Dedicating some time to meditation is a meaningful expression of caring for yourself that can help you move through the lire of feeling unworthy of recovery. As your mind grows quieter and more spacious, you can begin to see self-defeating thought patterns for what they are, and open to other, more positive options."

-Sharon Salzberg

Meditation is my favorite form of healing and it is so needed in the world. As part of your journey, consider adding forms of mediation to your everyday plans. I wake up and the first thing I do is a twenty-minute meditation. For me it is important to start my day grounded and ready to complete tasks. I have created a regimen that not only inspires me to be great, but it also makes me feel my best. My complete regimen is as follows:

1. Burn sage

2. Sit/lay down for a guided meditation

3. Pick a card from my goddess oracle cards

4. Read a daily declaration

5. Prayer

6. Write in my journal

7. Choose an oil and inhale deeply for clarity

8. Read my vision board and recite my daily affirmations aloud

The complete meditation takes me about an hour in the morning. This makes me so happy and keeps me at my best. You also have to remember what may work for me, may not work for you. Check in to see what part of the day will be the best time for you to meditate.

My favorite part of my morning routine is my connection to writing in my journal. I usually have a breakthrough every morning. I feel supported and loved by the universe. While most of the time I am happy, sometimes I may wake up feeing lonely. I usually then play some gospel music to restore my thinking and lead me to identify whatever I need support with. The step is another productive way to figure out who you are and want to be. I can identify my current connections with the universe as powerful and lifting.

Once your mind starts evolving, you will alter the people you attract. When you really figure out who you really are, you will be able to separate those in your life that have no meaning. You want to magnify the right people in your circle and release those who are with bad intentions and are not serving you.

Learning who you really are is probably one of the most difficult things you will do in your life, because you already put a label on yourself. You may say to yourself, *Oh, I'm a snob. Oh, I can't love anyone more than they love me. I don't deserve to be loved.* It's crazy what we talk ourselves into believing. We will sit on the couch all day whine and wince about our careers, family, friends, love lives, neighbors and strangers! But it's time to unlearn what you think is right and relearn what will elevate you.

Some people still don't know who they are and they're in their 60's, 70's, and older! Take your time to discover you deep down in your core and soul, then the love people will have for you can alter and move unwanted walls. You know what I mean, the wall that has been blocking your blessings. Treat your connection with the universe (God, Allah, Buddha, or your Higher Being) like it is the number one thing in your life that matters. Use meditation as a guiding light to remove fears from your mind.

Feeling centered and grounded creates a space for new things to happen in life so it important for me to tend to my self-care regimen each and every day. *Who would I be if I didn't have a morning ritual?* I already know: I'm impatient and I get easily annoyed. It is a defense mechanism that I have been using my entire life. When I am connected with my inner most self, I feel like I can take on the world being patient and vigorous.

Not sure how to meditate? Well grab some awesome tips from *YouTube*! As we all know, *YouTube* is the "Mecca" of video content and there are so many meditations that it would be impossible not to find one that speaks to you. Keep in mind that meditation can look different ways for different people. For instance, reading, cooking and cleaning are forms of meditation. How many times have you cleaned your house and thought, "My mind is clear now and I can think"? Listen to what can be defined as meditation to you and keep trying different things that inspire you to be the person who does what they are passionate about. Have what you've always wanted. Be. Do. Have.

If you are not communicating with the universe, then

the universe doesn't know how to support you. You may always feel like you are stuck in the same place with having nowhere else to go. Trust the process that you choose and be open to the possibilities of how your story can impact the world.

Remember the prayer I told God about not wanting a man in my life until this book was complete? Not only did I manifest this, but I cleared space to write this book without any distractions from a partner. I meditated without realizing how powerful my words were until this specific prayer. It is the reason why I have been celibate for over seven years.

Meditation is one of the steps where you will learn how to love yourself and understand your processes and how to shift your thinking. Meditation will keep your mind free. Exercising, yoga class, hiking, and deep breathing are other techniques to feel grounded. You know what they say, "whatever you put out into the universe is what you get back." Karma is the best example of this too. You know when you leave the house in the morning and it just feels like everything is going wrong? *Who are you being to attract the things that are showing up in your life?* Clear out emotions that don't service you in the morning so your day moves with ease.

For those of you who prefer to stick with guided meditations, I would also like to mention that bedtime meditations are an option as well. Before I go to bed, I usually pop my earphones in and search for a mantra that focuses on prosperity and wealth. *Did you know that your subconscious doesn't go to sleep?* Because of this, I enjoy listening to a meditation while I am sleeping to build new ideas that will help move me forward in life.

How will you know what works for you if you don't try? Add meditation to your daily routine and watch your life shift for the better. If you don't follow any other steps in this guide, let this one be your guiding force.

Exercise #8: Meditation is one of the most powerful tools to getting what you want in life. Write down some mantras below that will keep you motivated. Remember, meditation is the thought process of engaging in thought, contemplation or reflection.

· · · · 💋 · · · ·

_____

_____

_____

_____

_____

_____

_____

_____

_____

_____

_____

_____

_____

_____

_____

_____

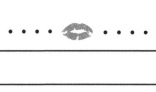

CHAPTER THIRTEEN

STEP NINE

DON'T FEEL GUILTY

"My alone feels good. I'll only have you if you are sweeter than my solitude."

-Warsan Shire

Celibacy is a voyage of healing and spirituality. I consider it a cleansing for the mind, body and soul or at least it has been for me. Celibacy puts you in control of your body and emotions. Celibacy is not a journey to be taken lightly. No matter the length of your journey, it is important to recognize the reasons for dedicating time into this space. For me, I decided I needed space after a bad breakup. During the first year through my journey, it seemed like the perfect solution to releasing baggage and pain so I stayed to myself. I would listen to music that inspired me like Mary J. Blige's, "Just Fine," Beyoncé's, "Best Thing I Never Had" and other R&B songs that invoked healing and femininity.

It was important for me to finish school above a 3.5 average just in case I wanted to go for my PhD in the future. It's been a wild ride. Six years of learning myself, loving myself, not blaming anyone for my shortcomings: just totally being with me. There were plenty of times I've bragged at celibacy and other times I felt like I was the only person in the world. You know what depression looks like: hours on end laying in the bed or couch and watching TV that doesn't touch, move, or inspire you at all. It is the type of depression that makes you second-guess your options in life like: *Why am I here? Will I ever be loved again? Who is going to love me feeling this way?*

If you are a virgin and decide to wait for sex because you want marriage, I think it's a great situation to be in as well. Don't rush it. Don't think, *Oh, because I'm 32, I need to now have sex before I turn 33. I should be married by now. I should have three kids, and be living in a house in the Hamptons.* No. That's not what sex is all about, and don't pressure yourself to do something that you will soon regret.

Don't allow others to make you feel guilty about your choice, especially those that know nothing about your journey. When you tell people that you are a virgin or celibate, they are eager to know why you would choose this. Some are genuinely curious and some just want to mock you. Stay away from people that bring negativity to your decision. If you have a partner who makes not having sex look like you are depriving him from getting love, then maybe you need a new relationship. You should be open to your partner in the first place about what is going on in your life. If they are willing to date you despite knowing you are not ready for sex, then they have no business guilt-tripping you into changing your mind. Remember intimacy is so much more than just sex.

I am very thankful for my life coach who has been able to create a platform for me that I didn't know that I had. I was able to build the goal of being complete and feeling enough during my commitment to celibacy. Because I am such a goal-getter, I've been creating and completing goals since

I was a little girl. But this was obviously the most difficult one, being that I've been sexually active in the past.

Guilt can quickly end your goals. Spend time digging into your core and working on the beliefs that you need and want in your life, the universe is waiting for your greatness!

Exercise #9: What forms of guilt could make you upset during this process of celibacy? Write down three or more examples and what action steps you need to eliminate the negative and step into the positive.

· · · · 👄 · · · ·

_____

_____

_____

_____

_____

_____

_____

_____

_____

_____

_____

_____

_____

_____

_____

_____

_____

_____

CHAPTER FOURTEEN

STEP TEN

HEALTH IS WEALTH

"It's not about perfect. It's about effort. And when you bring that effort every single day, that's where transformation happens. That's how change occurs."

-Jillian Michaels

In April 2016, I had to undergo my first major surgery. I was scheduled for a myomectomy because I had a 12cm fibroid, the size of a large grapefruit crushing my uterus. I always felt a mass near my pelvis but I thought it was backup waste (TMI I know.) When my holistic practitioner shared with me in November of 2015 I had a fibroid I was devastated. That evening, I had sleep paralysis for the third time in my life and I cried the night away.

After a couple of doctor visits I scheduled my surgery and I was excited to heal. During one of my appointments, the doctor asked me if I was sexually active. I shared no, and I have been celibate for six years. She looked at me and said, "I have something to share with you. Fibroids are built up estrogen that doesn't know where to go. Not having sex can be a part of the growth in your fibroid." I was in shock when she shared that information with me. I then asked, "If I started having sex again, would it shrink?" and she said no.

On the day of my surgery, I sat with my mom and friend as we sat patiently to be called into the operating room. As I made my way into the operating room, a tear dropped as I looked back at two very important people in my life. Once we passed the double doors and stepped into the operating room, I was amazed. Women physicians were ready to heal my womb! There wasn't one man in the room and I felt empowered as they made me feel comfortable and at ease. The anesthesiologist and I had the most fun in the room. She was petite but very powerful. I was amazed at her energy as she spoke to me, "Bernice, where do you want to travel to?" I told her, "Hawaii would be nice!" As she administered the "good stuff," I drifted off into "LaLa Land" and dreamt about the biggest ocean and the bluest sky.

After three days in the hospital, I arrived home and I was told that I had to be on bed rest for two weeks. Two weeks didn't sound like much until I had to do it. I spent two weeks binge watching different *Netflix* series and shows. I even had the time to watch *The Wire*, which was way too awesome. During my two weeks of bed rest and healing for a total of six weeks, I could not lift anything over 10 pounds. This interrupted my exercise regime. *What could I possibly do besides walking that would keep me moving?*

After I healed and started my workout regime again, I started to feel good mentally and spiritually. Exercise during celibacy is key. You need to keep your body well-balanced with nutrition and movement. Have you ever wondered why doctors prescribe exercise and nutritionists suggest healthy foods to keep your body active? Before celibacy, I wasn't that active. I would yo-yo with my weight (which honestly is happening now) but I now know the steps I need to be my best self. Exercise for me has been the best confidence booster ever! It has created a space of healing and releasing negative energy that doesn't support me.

Obesity and being overweight runs in my family. I've seen them struggle so I don't want to follow suit. My exercise regimen includes: *Zumba* classes, yoga, jogging in the park, and going out dancing with my friends. I make sure that I exercise at least three times every week and while I may struggle once in a while, I do my best to stick to a regime.

Guess what keeps me in check? Compliments! They keep me motivated to push on with my regime. Who doesn't like a juicy compliment while you're in the gym or leaving a yoga class? Looking and feeling good is one of the best ways to get your self-love on and if exercise and nutrition is going to get you there then, "Heyyyyyy mister trainer with the chocolate skin and toned body, how many sets again?"

When it comes to nutrition, spend your money on the good stuff. It may seem pricey for the time being but it can shift your life forever. Take my myomectomy surgery as an example to eat well. Remember food is not a replacement for sex, exercise is.

Two-step exercise :Exercise #10A: What are some of your favorite ways to release tension and make your body move? List different forms of exercises that you can add to your daily or weekly regimen.

· · · · 💋 · · · ·

_____

_____

_____

_____

_____

_____

_____

_____

_____

_____

_____

_____

_____

_____

_____

Exercise #10B: Review your eating habits and be honest: no one is judging you here. Are you eating a well-balanced diet? Make a list of your favorite foods and place a "√" next to the foods that are healthy. Now, place an "x" to the foods that are not as healthy. If 25% or more of your answers reveal an "x," it's time to shift your lifestyle.

• • • • 💋 • • • •

Part III: THE WAIT

CHAPTER FIFTEEN

REMEMBER THIS

Some things that you will experience on this journey will be exciting, while others will be damn frustrating. Check out this quick wrap up and jump into your celibacy journey with power!

1.   Be ready to shift... for the better

You know how you used to put so much effort and pay so much attention to your relationship and partner? During this journey you will notice that there has been a shift in your focus. That shift can be inward, which can support a spiritual goal or it could be outwards which can change your perception of how others treat you. Your reason for going on this journey in the first place will most likely be where your focus has shifted. It is a good thing because you get to achieve something outside of the norm, from self-discovery to spiritual clarity depending on what you want.

2.   You are more in tune with your emotions

Before this journey, I was so off balance with my emotions and I didn't know why. I finally have a grip on the things that I like and dislike. It has been one of my favorite reasons behind my experience that I love because I am clear on the things I will accept from a mate. The truth is you now know what you want and there is no such thing as settling for less. Self-love has grown heavily in this area and the people you care about most will see a whole new you with confidence seeping from every pore of your being.

3. It gives you a chance to start anew

Celibacy offers you a chance to start anew. It is so rewarding to release relationships that don't serve you. You will know yourself better and you will redefine your standards. You are no longer the person you used to be and you have the opportunity to open a different chapter in your life. Even if you had a rough start, you will go through the journey and decide what works best for you, it will keep you inspired to stretch and grow.

4. You acquire more discipline

Making a decision to be celibate is very challenging and requires great discipline to pull through. Just think of your favorite athlete, actor or leader. Their lives thrive through discipline. While celibacy cannot be directly compared to the previous titles, it is still honorary. I am happy to see the progress with my discipline though I still sometimes fluctuate with my weight. Learning the ways to grow through this form of discipline will support new goals and aspirations.

5. Companionship for the win!

"How sweet it is to be loved by you!" No seriously! My friendships have grown, my business has blossomed, my new sense of self is beautiful to look at and I can still work the room with flirting and not have to jump someone's bones! This experience has solidified companionship on an entirely new level. I no longer seek validation or permission from anyone and the relationships that mean the most to me are well spent enjoying each other's company.

CHAPTER SIXTEEN

SENDING MY LOVE

"Your journey will spark something new in you. Be brave. Be bold. Just be."

-Bernice Wooden

Facing the "rough patch" in my first year of celibacy and having friends around, especially my male friends to encourage me has kept me going longer than I thought I would. I feel blessed to be living the life I am living, especially the self-discovery that has come as a great reward. *What type of life would you have if there were no challenges? How would you move through and grow? How could you learn from mistakes and shift gears?* Imagine what would life be like if you didn't challenge yourself to trying a new recipe from a cookbook or challenging yourself by climbing a new heights?

One of my experiences back in Los Angeles, during my 30th birthday, included a hike through Runyon Canyon. At the time, I was working out consistently so my friend Laura asked me which route on the hike I wanted to take: easy, medium, or advanced. I was at a place in my life that I wanted the challenge so I chose advanced. As we climbed, she was much faster than I. She would patiently wait at rest stops as I did my best to catch up but would quickly fall behind.

The sun was becoming hotter and hotter each minute but I knew I had to continue the journey. There was absolutely no way I was turning back. Higher and higher we climbed, the more excited I was feeling. I created a space of victory before reaching the finish line. There was one part of the hike that was really challenging. And just when I was feeling great about finishing, there goes that damn stump in the road. It took me 10 minutes to garner up the strength and belief that I could climb the highest peak without falling. Imagine the things that were running through my mind: self-doubt, failure, and anger. I took a few deep breaths and made my way up the steep peak of the mountain. I made sure not to look down as I kept my body close to the hard rocks.

As I challenged myself, I kept my eyes on the top of the mountain and exuberance filled my body. As I took the final step up the steep mound of foundation I shouted for joy! It was one of the most profound feelings in my life! And you know what made it even more special? I, Bernice Wooden, was at the highest peak of the Canyon and saw the most beautiful views I've ever seen. While the air was thick and muggy from the heat, imagine Los Angeles at 11 a.m. in August, I sat on one of the rocks and just smiled. I was expecting tears of joy but my heart was set on the magnificent sky and landscape. It was then where I believed more than ever that I could do anything I set my mind to.

If you ever wondered, yes, I am sex positive. While I am choosing to refrain from sexual intercourse, I am still that vivacious woman who enjoys hearing her friends talk about sex every chance I can get. It's not like I am fishing for stories, but when my girlfriends share that they had an amazing experience, I want to hear every detail. It gets me all the more excited for my next encounter. I know it will be powerful and amazing.

I would have never fathomed the idea that I would be celibate from 26 years old to the present. As I continue to grow powerfully day-by-day, I have created so many new relationships that I adore and admire. From new business ventures to even writing this book would have been a, "yeah right" in my mind. With everything in life, you get to choose who you will be: passive or proactive. What are you choosing?

As I continue on this journey of celibacy, I want to leave you with these final words: Set your goals with intention and grace. If you fail, learn from the lesson and try again. What makes this life so amazing are the opportunities for growth and strength. I have faced many challenges in life but I know adversity only makes you stronger. My journey has equipped me with life-long lessons of gratitude, forgiveness and persistence. No one is going to value you any less than what you've set your goals on. Use the steps in this book to create a space of love, joy, and healing for yourself. I am no longer bound by the need to "look good" and to receive validation. I am living my life on my own terms and I'm creating memories that will last a lifetime. As you continue to love through the universe, remember one thing: **JUST BE.**

The Finale: Use the remaining blank spaces to release any emotions you have around celibacy and/or sex. Reflect and grow.

NATURE'S NOTE

The sun is the brightest star in the universe.

It shines effortlessly between the clouds and blue skies.

It reflects power and demands attention.

It brightens the green grass to a shade of wholeness and vibrancy.

The sun warms your soul and supports a healthy body with an unlimited supply of Vitamin D.

It is a source of joy and laughter.

The sun reminds us each and every morning to smile; it is the perfect wake up call.

The sun keeps us alive while moving through life at peace and whenever the sun is too strong, grab some shade under a full tree.

Learn to be the sun.

~~The sun~~ Bernice is the brightest star in the universe.

~~It~~ I shine~~s~~ effortlessly between the clouds and blue skies.

~~It~~ reflect~~s~~ power and I demand~~s~~ attention.

~~It~~ brighten~~s~~ ~~the green grass~~ myself to a shade of wholeness and vibrancy.

~~The sun~~ I warm~~s~~ ~~you're~~ my soul and support~~s~~ a healthy body with an unlimited supply of Vitamin D.

~~It is~~ I am a source of joy and laughter.

~~The sun~~ I reminds ~~us~~ myself each and every morning to smile; ~~it is~~ I am the perfect wake up call.

~~The sun~~ I keeps ~~us~~ myself alive while moving through life at peace and whenever the sun is too strong, I will grab some shade under a full tree.

Learn to be the sun.

Acknowledgements

Whew! I can't believe I did it! I have been sitting on this book for four years. *Four years of uncertainty and what if's? How will this book affect my future intimate relationships? What fears around being celibate kept my secret bottled up inside?* I not only feel relieved and overjoyed but I feel renewed and restored. Nothing is more invigorating than stepping outside of your shell and speaking your truth.

I would like to thank my Mom. You have guided me the best way you could and I am forever grateful. Your lessons not only inspire me but also those who have been able to sit in your presence. Nothing is more powerful than seeing a woman speak her truth without a care in the world. Continue being perfectly imperfect.

Dad. We've never met but it is important for me to acknowledge you. You see, there were many times that I could have blamed you for the things that were missing in my life and sometimes I did. However, you being absent gave my mother permission to teach me how to be independent, an entrepreneur and a leader and for that I appreciate you.

My exes. I want to thank each and every one of you from the bottom of my heart for teaching me the truth about myself. I never would have written this story if it wasn't for our up's and down's. Sharing parts of our experiences continue to guide me to stand strong in my intentions and expectations for my next relationship.

Goddesses, friends and to my 4's... **WHERE WOULD I BE** if your love, accountability and community didn't push me? I am so grateful to those you have contributed to the completion of this book. You know who you are!

I would also like to thank my team on this book project: Demarcus McGaughey, Elizabeth David Dembrowsky, Danielle Fontus, Charon Richardson, Ryan "Skye" Washington, Camella Fairweather, Lauren Varlack, Sandra Lopez-Monsalve, Juana Guichardo, Diamond Pendelton and Xanda Tonge. I am truly in debt to all of you as your professionalism kept me in check and carried me through. Thank you.

God. I've prayed for your guidance and approval for years but you would always say, "Trust yourself and everything is going to be alright." I get it now. The morning after I dreamt about the title of this book and before the idea of writing it came into fruition, I was in awe and pretty scared that this could happen. Thank you for pushing me past my fears. My life has expanded through leaps and bounds, may your love continue to shine through universe and me.

About the Author

Bernice Wooden is the Founder and CEO of *Be Nice Productions.* She creates love and joy through innovative forms of entertainment. If it's hosting networking workshops in New York City, being hired at the United Nations as a videographer for the Nigerian Embassy, or taking portraits of entrepreneurs: she does it all. Clients include: *Panasonic, Visa, Procter and Gamble, SL Green Reality Corp.* amongst many others. She enjoys building authentic relationships and spending time traveling the world. She currently lives in Brooklyn, New York.